Saint Michael the Archangel

Devotion, Prayers & Living Wisdom

Edited by Mirabai Starr

EasyRead Large

Copyright Page from the Original Book

Sounds True, Inc., Boulder, CO 80306

© 2007 Mirabai Starr

SOUNDS TRUE is a trademark of Sounds True, Inc. All rights reserved. No part of this book may be used or reproduced in any manner without written permission from the author and publisher.

Published 2007
ISBN 978-1-59179-627-5

Library of Congress Cataloging-in-Publication Data

Saint Michael the Archangel : devotions, prayers, and living wisdom / [compiled by] Mirabai Starr.
    p. cm.—(Devotions, prayers, and living wisdom series ; bk. 2)
    Includes bibliographical references (p. 117).
    ISBN 978-1-59179-627-5 (hardcover)
1. Michael (Archangel)—Prayers and devotions. I. Starr, Mirabai.
BT968.M5S25 2007
235'.3—dc22
                            2007031066

For a free catalog of wisdom teachings for the inner life, call (800) 333-9185 or visit www.soundstrue.com.

Digital Edition 12/09

ISBN: 978-1-59179-865-1

TABLE OF CONTENTS

Also in this Series	i
Publisher's Note	ii
Editor's Note	iii
Opening Prayer	vii
Introduction	ix
Chapter One: Strength and Protection	1
Chapter Two: The Calling	28
Chapter Three: Guardian of Souls	51
Chapter Four: Compassion	63
Closing Prayer	79
Sources	81
Bibliography	86
Credits	88
About Sounds True	91
Front Cover Flap	92
Back Cover Flap	93
Back Cover Material	94

Also in this Series

Saint Francis of Assisi
Saint Teresa of Avila
Hildegard of Bingen
Our Lady of Guadalupe
Saint John of the Cross

Publisher's Note

Sounds True's *Devotions, Prayers, and Living Wisdom* series began with a desire to offer the essential teachings of great saints, mystics, and spiritual figures in a format that is compatible with meditation and contemplation. Each book contains poems, prayers, songs, and prose written by or in veneration of a figure who has transcended human confusion, and whose wisdom might awaken our own. It is our hope that these books will offer you insight, renewal, and companionship on the spiritual path.

Editor's Note

I am a committed pacifist. And I don't believe in a personified devil or even an external force that might be called evil. So I was not immediately drawn to the Archangel Michael, famous for charging forth with sword uplifted to smite the Enemy in the name of God.

As I delved deeper into the Michael material, however, two things struck me and expanded my perspective on this important figure. First, Michael represents the Spiritual Warrior inside each of us, who, with unconditional love in his heart, is willing to stand up for what he believes is right. Second, the weapon Michael wields is what the Buddhists refer to as the Sword of Discrimination, which cuts through illusion and lays the truth bare. Who couldn't use a dose of this medicine?

Because Michael is a supernatural being and therefore did not write, I have relied on prayers and poems written to him, and scriptural passages and personal testimonies about him.

The list at the back of the book identifies the diverse sources I drew from to compile these selections. When I found references to Michael's hand in well-known biblical events, I had a great deal of fun elaborating in my own versions. My personal reflections and stories are distinguished by italics in the text.

This book is divided into four chapters, reflecting the major themes I uncovered as I explored the writings I encountered about Michael: the power of strength and protection in times of danger; the divine assistance that comes when we are called upon to do acts of great service in the world; the shepherding of souls through death to the afterlife; and the quality of mercy and compassion implicit in Michael's defense of the innocent.

May this collection of devotional jewels help you cultivate the courage and clarity you need in your own life, so that you may transcend whatever forces of darkness prevent you from finding true inner peace, thereby increasing your ability to contribute to a more peaceful world.

I am deeply grateful for the generous contributions and wise counsel of Father William Hart McNichols, Professor Larry Torres, Jennifer Paulden, Scott, Ruby Martinez, Nancy Casey, Sarah Jane Freymann, Kelly Notaras, and Haven Iverson.

—Mirabai Starr
June 2007

Image A

Opening Prayer

Praise to you,
Archangel Michael,
you who appeared to the ancient prophets
and helped them rise to the station of
their sacred calling
so that they could serve the Divine
with courage and loyalty.
Make us all prophets, now.

In times of grave danger
you come with sword uplifted
to cut through the darkness and banish illusion.
Society is in turmoil and the earth is in peril.
Give us the strength and clarity
to effect conscious, loving change
in this troubled world
and inside our own souls.

Thank you.
Amen.

—Mirabai Starr

Image B

Introduction

The Spiritual Warrior

Michael the Archangel is the prototype for the virtues of the spiritual warrior, a paradigm we find at the heart of every spiritual tradition.

The spiritual warrior is committed to non-violence in all his relationships. The conflict he engages in is the battle within. This is the struggle to discern his true calling from the endless stream of life's distractions. It requires great courage and forbearance to step onto the inner battlefield and strike down whatever internal demons stand between our real self and our false self.

The spiritual warrior is the most peaceful person in the community. Because he has dedicated himself to truth at all costs, he is incapable of engaging in any behavior that creates misunderstanding or strife. He is the champion of those who suffer and the protector of those who long to be free. In ancient England, he is represented by Saint George, the legendary dragon slayer.

The only legitimate war, says the Qur'an, is the war between the forces of good and evil inside ourselves. This is called the "inner jihad." *Jihad* means "to strive." We never stop striving to overcome our own negativity and to live righteously. This view challenges the bias we so often encounter when the media attempts to define Islam.

The spiritual warrior wields the sword of discrimination. With this weapon always at his side, he is ready to cut through illusion and liberate that which is real. He is never unkind, but he is not always gentle. He is perpetually honing his blade, and his powers of detection are sharp. When he perceives falsehood, he names it, and then he destroys it. He is not afraid. He has nothing to lose.

When we call upon the spirit of Michael, we are invoking the courage and strength to see the truth and live it, to hear the truth and share it, to know the truth and let it change us.

We fearlessly fling open the doors of our own conscience and examine what we find there. Where we see petty jealousy, we smite it. Where we see irritability toward the people with whom we share our lives, we banish it. Where we see selfishness, indolence, and cynicism, we cut them out of our hearts.

And yet we must always practice compassion toward our adversary: we must forgive ourselves.

Where we see kindness, let us tenderly cultivate it. Where we see playfulness and joy, let us protect it. Where we see self-appreciation, let us embrace it. Wherever there is love, let us hold a feast in its honor.

***

In Hebrew, the name "Michael" means "who is like God?" This evokes Exodus 15:11: "Who is like to you among the gods, O Lord? Who is like to you, magnificent in holiness?"

Michael embodies the spirit of inquiry. With his sword of discrimination, Michael continuously cuts through the layers of illusion to uncover the truth. He never ceases to question reality.

Is there any other god but God? Do our efforts to define the Divine, to enumerate its attributes and explain its functions, violate its essential unity and sovereignty? Does naming the Holy One diminish the Holy One?

Have we engaged in activities we have elevated to such exalted status that they have replaced God in our lives? Are we worshipping money and the objects money can buy? Have we made substances our gods, and addiction our primary form of devotion? Maybe we feel trapped in an abusive relationship whereby our life-force is diminished every day. We can ask to borrow Michael's sword and cut through the tentacles we have wrapped around our lives.

Have we resigned ourselves to allowing injustice to unfold in a situation over which we feel we have no control? If we ask Michael, he will show us that we not only have the power but the obligation to stand up for the rights of the oppressed.

Have we been reluctant to excavate our souls and psyches for fear of the darkness we might find there? If we call on him, Michael will infuse us with courage and strength to enter the interior wilderness and banish the demons that keep us on the periphery of an authentic existence.

Michael invites us to cultivate our curiosity and challenge ourselves to place the Divine at the center of everything we do and everything we are.

***

Michael is also the angel to whom the Holy One assigned the task of delivering the souls of the deceased to the heavenly realms. The Archangel fulfills his role with unutterable tenderness and respect. This has earned Michael the love of people of faith from diverse spiritual traditions throughout time.

Because of his devotion to returning the souls of humanity back to their divine source, the Catholic Church honors the Archangel with the title of Saint. Michael is not canonized because he never died. Yet, like a human saint, the Archangel Michael stands for the people. We feel close to him. We look to him to intercede on our behalf.

Defend Us

Michael is the angel of protection. He is invoked in times of danger. Whenever we feel the spirit of evil playing around the edges of our world, we may call on the Archangel Michael to surround us with a shield of divine light to keep us safe from harm.

Michael is the Angel of the Lord in the Hebrew Bible, who guided the Israelites through the wilderness. In the Roman Catholic liturgy, Saint Michael is the patron saint of the military and the police force. According to Muslims, the archangels are so holy their form is impossible to behold.

Michael's mission is more global than personal. Throughout the ages, the Archangel has appeared in support of those human beings who are taking on some vast task on behalf of humanity, such as Abraham, Sarah, Moses, and Joan of Arc.

***

According to the legends of the Abrahamic tradition, before the Holy One created earth and all its creatures, he created the angels in heaven, with the sole task of adoring him. This was not arrogance; it was love. The angelic choirs could do nothing but echo God's love back to him. The dazzling radiance of the angelic forms could only mirror the radiant love of the Divine.

And so all the angels bowed down to the Holy One in ecstatic reverence. All except for one angel, who refused to worship him: the one they called Lucifer, bearer of divine light, originally the most luminous angel of all. And Lucifer corrupted lesser spirits, seducing them away from the Divine with false promises.

The Holy One appointed the Archangel Michael, the embodiment of strength and the spirit of protection, to cast Lucifer out of heaven. As Michael engaged Lucifer in battle, the rebel angel took the form of a fire-breathing dragon, and the archangel took the form of a knight in shining armor. Michael fought single-handedly, while

Lucifer was flanked by an entourage of evil spirits.

They fought a tremendous battle at the gates of heaven. Michael, the more virtuous opponent, prevailed. He crushed Lucifer beneath his feet and hurled him down to hell. And he chained the evil spirits in midair.

From their vantage point between heaven and earth, the fallen angels could see the glory of paradise spread above them and the wonderment of creation unfold below. To witness these blessings and be unable to participate was a grave punishment.

It is said that the spirit of evil feeds on frustration. It yearns to fully engage with life, to create beauty, to have fun, to taste everything. But it cannot allow itself to do so.

One day, some accounts promise, the Holy One will remember his prisoners and set them free. They will be reformed and they will radiate divine love everywhere—in heaven and on earth and through all the forgotten chambers of the hell realms.

Ruby

Ruby Martinez is the single mother of a sixteen-year-old son named Joaquin. Her husband, Juan de la Cruz, died when Joaquin was nine.

Every year for the past three centuries, Ruby's small community in northern New Mexico holds a weekend celebration in honor of the feast days of Santiago and Santa Ana in July. During "fiestas," the generations mingle and attend Mass together, and people of all ages enjoy the parade, the food, the traditional costumes, and the music that fill the historic town plaza.

Last summer, Joaquin decided to go to a late movie with his friends after fiestas. Ruby agreed. When the movie was over, Joaquin called to tell his mom that he and his friends were on their way home.

"I don't have a good feeling about you being out so late during fiestas," Ruby said. "There are crazy drivers out there tonight."

"We'll take the back roads," Joaquin assured his mom.

When she hung up the phone, Ruby did something she had never done before. She dropped to her knees and called on Saint Michael, uttering the prayer of protection Juan had taught her, pleading with the Archangel to keep their son safe.

"You don't invoke San Miguel lightly," Ruby says. "Your need has to be really strong to ask for his help. Michael is about protection against evil. I don't know exactly what made me think my son was in need of the intercession of San Miguel that night, but the feeling was so strong I couldn't ignore it."

As Ruby prayed, a sense of profound peace and well-being washed over her. She sat in quiet meditation late into the night, until the phone rang. It was Joaquin's friend.

"There's been an accident but everyone's okay," he said in a rush before Ruby would have time to panic. "Someone's coming to pick us up, and they'll drop Joaquin off at home."

Joaquin walked through the door a little while later, expecting his mother to be hysterical. Instead, Ruby was completely calm. She took him into the bathroom and examined the small cuts on his face, then washed them and applied ointment.

Joaquin told his mother that the car had rolled several times and both back tires had blown out. "All I remember is closing my eyes and falling through space," Joaquin said. "We should all be dead."

But Joaquin's minor abrasions represented the full extent of the injuries involved. The car was totaled.

"You had some powerful angels on your side tonight, son," Ruby said.

Earlier that same summer, Joaquin had traveled to Miami to visit his sister, who was living there. He had returned with a tattoo of the archangel Michael battling *el Diablo* on his arm. He braced himself for his mother's displeasure, but, to his amazement, Ruby was not upset. Instead, she chose that moment to disclose an important aspect of Joaquin's spiritual legacy: "San Miguel was your father's patron saint," she informed her son. It was as if Joaquin had a premonition of the danger he would soon face.

The night of the accident, Ruby felt the spirit of her husband and the protective power of the Archangel Michael enfolding Joaquin in their collective embrace, keeping him safe from harm. Incomparably grateful, she gave thanks.

Jenna

Jenna Paulden is a teacher at a Waldorf School, part of an international alternative educational system, founded by the Austrian philosopher, Rudolf Steiner. Saint Michael was a primary inspiration and guide for Steiner, who felt that Michael holds the key to planetary transformation and balance. Along with the rest of the angelic kingdom, Michael infuses the heart of the Waldorf curriculum.

When Jenna first began teaching, she was already deeply acquainted with the unseen realms. She had always invoked *devas* and other nature spirits to nurture her lush mountain garden. It was natural for her to turn to Michael for guidance in the classroom. Her primary issue had to do with holding her authority with unruly children.

"My question was, how do I maintain a space of unconditional love and deal with children who may be asking for boundaries in some very rude ways?" Jenna says. "I knew I needed to give them clear limits without getting angry or coming from a place of frustration and control."

Jenna says Michael reminded her that the warrior stance is not one of attack-defense and that the sword he carries is the sword of unconditional love. It's a position held with such depth and breadth that there is no room for anything but love.

"Michael also helped me cut away all the garbage I had attached to my authority, the stuff that came up when I felt my power was being threatened. He enabled me to visualize the sword. It's not a 'kill the bad guys' kind of sword. It's the sword of truth. And the truth is love."

But the sword of truth is not enough. "Michael has a consort and her name is Faith," Jenna adds. "How are you going to use that sword unless you have faith that it's real and that you're capable of using it?"

With Michael at her side, Jenna feels empowered to walk into the classroom and face her own preconceptions about leadership as she strives to set healthy boundaries and meet her students' behaviors with love.

"Michael is helping me create a crucible of creative learning and a whole new consciousness," Jenna says. "The transformation happens through my guise of being a teacher, and the children's guise of having their little issues, but it's much bigger than that."

Mark

Mark and his first wife were divorced when their son Sam was two. When Sam was three, Mark married Sarah, a non-denominational minister who shared Mark's eclectic beliefs and interest in spiritual healing. Soon after, Mark's ex-wife relocated with their son from Arizona to Washington and enrolled him in a private pre-school.

Soon after entering the program, Sam began to display signs of ritual abuse. His mother placed him in psychological counseling and imposed severe restrictions on Sam's visitation with his father and stepmother.

After struggling for a year and a half to regain access to his son, Mark finally had liberal rights restored. Sam immediately confided in his father and stepmother about the strange and scary experiences he had been having at his pre-school. It became clear to them that this was the source of the psychological problems Sam was having.

Mark and Sarah reported their suspicions to Social Services. Troubled by the agency's complete lack of response, Mark then contacted local law enforcement. When the police went to the school to investigate allegations of ritual abuse, the school had scrambled to remove any evidence of Satanic worship.

Frustrated, but unwilling to back down, Mark and Sarah launched an independent investigation. They even solicited the support of the FBI. As the couple gathered photographs, children's drawings and testimonials from current and past students, it became apparent to them that the school was operated by a Satanic cult, part of a vast network of preschools designed to indoctrinate children by committing horrific acts of physical, sexual, and emotional violence against them.

As the evidence unfolded, Mark and Sarah began to notice that they were being followed wherever they went. Pseudo-repairmen would come to their hotel room at odd hours to install unexplained devices. When they ordered a pizza, a deliveryman arrived immediately. Suspicious, Mark and Sarah threw the food away, only to have the real order show up minutes later.

They endured loud whispers all night in the hallways while figures dressed in black continuously filed in and out of adjoining rooms. They found explosives in their rental car. Mark and Sarah were afraid to eat, afraid to sleep, afraid to leave their hotel room.

One morning, as the couple prepared to meet with Sam's therapist and confront her, Sarah told Mark that she didn't think she could face this next encounter. They strongly suspected that the therapist was a member of the same organization that ran the school.

Sarah had been working tirelessly on Sam's behalf. She had engaged a wide circle of friends all over the world who she referred to as "light workers" to pray for the child throughout the investigation. She had been by Mark's side during every step of the long ordeal. Lack of sleep and inadequate nutrition had finally exhausted her.

Mark reassured Sarah that he would be fine on his own and he left the hotel alone. He saw men and women dressed in the same black outfits milling around both sides of the street. Taking a deep breath, he began to walk toward the therapist's office.

Suddenly, Mark felt a powerful, protective presence beside him. He caught a glimpse of a towering figure carrying an enormous sword. He knew instantly that it was the archangel Michael. In that moment, all Mark's fear unraveled and he was completely calm and confident. As he strode down the street, Mark reports, the stalkers scattered like cockroaches under a bright light. He was never afraid again.

Shortly after Mark's visitation from Michael, the pre-school was shut down and Sam's healthy and happy relationship with his father and stepmother was restored. Mark realized that the work he and Sarah had done to uncover what turned out to be an extensive ring of ritual child abuse was not only a matter of protecting their own family. The archangel Michael came to their aid because they had engaged in a fundamental battle between the forces of darkness and light.

Apparitions and Shrines

Michael made several dramatic appearances in ancient history. In the third century, Emperor Constantine claimed that Michael appeared to him in the sky above Constantinople, brandishing a sword and a cross, on the eve of his battle against a rival emperor for control of the Roman Empire. Constantine's subsequent victory on the battlefield represented Christ's victory over Constantine's soul: in that moment, the emperor became a Christian convert.

Michael is known not only as the angel of protection, but also as the angel of healing. In the seventh century, when Rome was being decimated by the plague, Pope Gregory prayed to Saint Michael to lift the curse from the people. Gregory led the Roman people in a holy procession through the streets for three days. When they reached the tomb of Emperor Hadrian, Michael appeared over Hadrian's grave, his sword dripping with blood, and the sickness soon passed from the city. Gregory built a church at the site of Hadrian's mausoleum and named it *Castel Sant'Angelo,* or "Castle of the Holy Angel."

Phrygia, in Asia Minor, has a long history of venerating angels. It is said that in the first century, Michael caused a healing spring to flow from the barren rocks at Colossae in Phrygia. Pilgrims suffering from disease and disabilities made their way to churches dedicated to the Archangel Michael throughout the region, seeking, and finding, miraculous cures.

At the end of the sixth century, Michael appeared to a wealthy man named Gargano in southern Italy. One day, a lone bull strayed from Gargano's large herd. Gargano sent a servant to look for the errant creature. The man found the bull at the entrance to a cave.

Infuriated by having had to waste so much time and energy looking for an animal, Gargano ordered his servant to kill the bull. But when the man aimed and shot his arrow, it reversed its trajectory in midair and struck him through the heart, killing him instantly.

Gargano was deeply distressed. He sought the advice of the local bishop, who entered a state of prayer and fasting. After three days, Michael appeared to the bishop in a vision. The Archangel descended to earth on the spot where the bull had been found. He told the bishop that the servant had been sacrificed as a sign of the holiness of this place, and a shrine to Saint Michael must be built there.

When Gargano and the bishop went to the cave the following day, they found three lavish altars inside. A stream of pure water flowed from a rock and was soon found to have healing properties. Monte Gargano continues to be a popular pilgrimage site to this day.

In the eighth century, Bishop Aubert of Avranches had a vision of Saint Michael that also involved a bull. Just off the coast of Normandy is a huge rock that turns into an island at high tide. One night, the Archangel appeared to Aubert and told him to go to the highest point of the rock, where he would find an area trampled by the hoofprints of an invisible bull, as well as a spring of healing waters. He was to build a shrine to Saint Michael on that spot.

Aubert dismissed the vision as a dream. But it came again. And again. On the third visitation, Michael touched the bishop's forehead with his angelic thumb, searing a print that remained for the rest of Aubert's life. The next day, Aubert visited the island and arranged to have a church erected there immediately. Visitors still flock to the sanctuary of Mont San Michel during high tide every day.

In the Middle Ages, a thirteen-year-old girl from France,

named Joan, began hearing the voice of an angel, who finally appeared in full form, surrounded by a host of other angels. It was Saint Michael. He was young, strong, and radiantly handsome. He told Joan that God had chosen her to liberate the French people from domination by England. He instructed her in every detail of the battle she was to lead.

Before Joan was burned at the stake as a heretic, she testified that Saint Michael the Archangel had guided her every step. The judges did not believe her. St. Joan of Arc was martyred in 1431 at the age of nineteen.

In more recent history, the elderly Pope Leo XIII collapsed during a meeting with his cardinals. The physicians who rushed to revive him could not detect a pulse and assumed that he had died. But after a few minutes, the pope opened his eyes and described a terrifying vision he had just experienced.

Pope Leo saw a host of evil spirits working diligently to undermine everything that is holy in this world. Just when the visionary was about to despair, the Archangel Michael appeared and vanquished the Prince of Darkness and his helpers, hurling them back to the underworld. After his recovery, the pope wrote a prayer to Saint Michael, which was recited at the end of mass in Catholic churches all over the world from the early nineteenth century until the 1960s.

While Michael has historically limited his exalted appearance to celebrated servants of humanity during times of global crisis, people of all statures and spiritual orientations have reported a very personal sense of connection with the Archangel in the face of great danger. Michael medicine is powerful, and not to be taken casually. But when the need is strong, turning to Michael could be the perfect remedy.

xxxii

Image C

Chapter One

Strength and Protection

The Strongest Woman in the World

The strongest woman in the world is ready to die.

"Michael," the Christ calls to the archangel. "As your brother Gabriel went to my mother and alerted her of my impending birth, please, go now and advise her that her death is approaching."

And the passing of the Blessed Mother shall be as immaculate as the conception of the Christ.

The archangel descends through the seven gateways and appears at Mary's feet as she spins flax in the doorway of her hermitage. She looks up from her work, peers into the light of the setting sun. His wings are glimmering; his eyes, filled with mercy.

"My Queen."

"Michael. Is it time?"

"Soon, your Majesty."

"Thank you, my angel." He kneels and she touches his face. "And what will happen to God's House when I am gone?" she asks.

"The men will storm the gates," Michael admits. "They will not stay forever. But while they are there, they will relegate you to the status of sweet victim. They will call you 'Mary, meek and mild.'"

The Blessed Mother tilts back her head and laughs.

Mary, meek and mild.

Who was it that sat up straight in bed when the fearsome Archangel Gabriel appeared in her room? Who did not cry out but listened carefully when he explained that the Holy Spirit would come after him, would enter her and fill her and quicken her with life, with the Life of Life, with life disguised as death, with the Word of God disguised as a child? Who understood the unbearable suffering to come and took a deep breath in the dark and said, "Yes."

Mary.

And it was Mary who labored in the storm to give birth to the Word of God. Mary who bore silent witness to each miracle. Mary who followed her son up Golgotha Hill as he struggled, beaten and bleeding, under the impossible weight of his own gallows. Mary who stood beside him as the guards drove iron stakes into his hands and feet—Mary whose heart was pierced with each blow of the mallet.

The strongest woman in the world.

And it was Mary who did not turn away from his pain when they hoisted the crossed timbers into the noonday sun and left him there to suffocate in the fluids that slowly filled his lungs. Mary who sang to him the Hebrew lullabies of his childhood and hers. Mary who promised to stay with him until he fell asleep.

Mary who enfolded his grieving disciples as her own sons after he had died and risen again and ascended and was gone.

The strongest woman in the world folds her yarn into a loose skein and sets it on the bench beside her. Michael sits quietly beneath the cypress tree in the courtyard. Mary inhales the cool desert air. Exhales luxuriously. Her heart leaps in a surge of excitement. Like a child about to embark on a voyage. Like a bride about to enter the chamber of her beloved on their wedding night.

"Yes," she says again. Says yes to Michael as she had said yes to Gabriel all those years ago. "Yes" as she had said yes when she held her son's lifeless head in her lap after they cut him from the cross. Exactly as she had said yes the morning after the Sabbath, when the rock was rolled away and his body had disappeared from its tomb.

"Yes," meaning, "I am ready." Meaning ... "Thy will, not mine, be done."

At dawn, as the village prepares to meet the day, Mary props her staff against the open door and then steps out into the road. She cups her hands and lifts them in offering.

And the Archangel Michael, invisible to everyone but her, gathers her body into his arms and rises with it high into the morning air. The villagers stand in *awe as Mary ascends, robes fluttering, face resplendent, and vanishes.*

The strongest woman in the world has gone home.

***

> St. Michael, the archangel of God,
> please be with us to help us
> at the moment of our terrible fight.
> Protect and save us
> from the tricks and evils of Satan.
> We pray humbly
> that God might scold Satan.
> Oh! Heavenly commander of armies,
> with the power of God,
> you push all the evil spirits and Satan,
> who are wandering everywhere to destroy souls,
> into the heavenly fire.
> Amen.
>
> —traditional Catholic prayer,
> translated by Father Emmanuel Kaniamparampil,
> a Carmelite priest from Kerala, India, from
> his native language of Malayalam

***

O glorious archangel, Saint Michael,
Prince of the heavenly host,
be our defense
in the terrible battle we carry on
against the powers of darkness,
against the rulers of this dark world,
against the evil spirits.

Come to the aid of humanity,
whom the Divine has created
in its own image
and ransomed at a great price
from the tyranny of the spirit of evil.

Join the holy angels today
and fight the Lord's fight,
as you have already fought
the leader of the angels of pride,
who were powerless to resist you,
whom you banished
from their place in heaven.

You cast that ancient cruel spirit
who seduces the whole world
into the abyss

along with his angels.

Behold.
This primeval adversary and slayer of humanity
has taken courage.
Disguised as an angel of light,
he wanders the land with his multitude of evil spirits,
invading the earth,
trying to blot out the name of the Holy One,
trying to seize and destroy souls destined
to receive the crown of eternal glory
and cast them into eternal perdition.

This wicked dragon pours out his malice
in a vile flood of venom
on those who are weakened by
a warped mind and a corrupt heart.
He poisons them
with the fetid breath of iniquity,
with the spirit of lying,
with sacrilege and irreverence,

with every vice and addiction.

These incredibly crafty adversaries
have infiltrated the House of God.
They have inebriated the inhabitants
with bitterness and cynicism.
They have compromised the integrity
of the beloved of the immaculate lamb,
and laid their foul hands
on her most sacred possessions.

In the Holy Place itself,
they have removed the Chair of Truth,
reserved for the Light of the World,
and replaced it
with the throne of their abomination.
Their evil design is to strike the shepherd
and scatter the sheep.

Rise up, then, invincible Prince!
Defend the people of God
against the attacks of the lost spirits.

Give them victory.
They venerate you
as their guardian and protector.
The House of God has proclaimed you
her defense against the
malicious power of darkness.
God has entrusted to you
the souls of humanity
so that you may lift them
into the heavenly light.

Oh, pray that the God of Peace
help us to put the spirit of evil
beneath our feet.
Let us so thoroughly disempower him
that he will never again be able
to violate God's House
and hold us captive.
Deliver our prayers
into the sight of the Most High
so that they may swiftly
merit his mercy.

Beat down the dragon,
that ancient serpent,
who is the embodiment of evil.
Exile him to the abyss

so that he may never again
lead the nations astray.

>   —adapted Catholic prayer

***

Glorious Saint Michael,
Prince of the heavenly hosts,
who stands always ready
to give assistance
to the people of God;
who fought with the dragon,
the old serpent,
and cast him out of heaven,
and now valiantly defends
the House of God
that the gates of hell
may never prevail against her,
I earnestly entreat you
to assist me also,
in the painful and dangerous
conflict
that I sustain
against the same formidable foe.

Be with me, O mighty Prince!
that I may courageously fight
and vanquish that proud spirit,

whom you, by the Divine Power,
gloriously overthrew,
and whom our powerful King, Jesus Christ,
has, in our nature,
completely overcome;
so having triumphed
over the enemy of my salvation,
I may, with you and the holy angels,
praise the clemency of God, who,
having withheld pity
from the rebellious angels
after their fall,
has granted repentance and forgiveness
to fallen humanity.

Amen.

—traditional Catholic prayer, "Prayer for Help Against Spiritual Enemies"

***

O Word of God!
Life-spring of the soul!
Power of the Beloved!

Bright glory!

We join the angels
in singing your praises.
The angels draw
their light and life
from you.

Your numberless multitudes
are spread poised
across the blue arc of the sky.
Michael raises your flag
and lifts your mighty cross
on high.

With that single gesture,
he banished the dragon prince
and all his rebel powers.
They tumbled like thunderbolts
from the high towers of heaven
into the underworld.

Help us, O Lord,
to stand with Michael
and continue to fight
against the prince of pride,
so that when we kneel before
the Lamb's pure throne of light,
we may be worthy

to receive his crown.

Praise be to God,
Who has redeemed us with the Holy Word;
Who has anointed us with the Holy Spirit;
Who guards us with the angel-host.

Amen.

—adapted Catholic hymn from the Office of St. Michael

***

Then war broke out in heaven; Michael and his angels battled against the dragon. The dragon and its angels fought back, but they did not prevail, and there was no longer any place for them in heaven.

The huge dragon, the ancient serpent, who is called the Devil and Satan, who deceived the whole world, was thrown down to earth, and its angels were thrown down with it.

—Revelation 12:7-8

***

Most glorious Prince of the Heavenly host,
Saint Michael the Archangel,
defend us in our battle against principalities and powers,
against the rulers of this world of darkness,
against the spirit of wickedness in the high places.

Come to the assistance of human beings,
whom God has created to His likeness
and whom He has redeemed at a great price
from the tyranny of the spirit of evil.

The Holy House of God venerates you
as her guardian and protector;
to you the Lord has entrusted
the souls of the redeemed
to be led into Paradise.

Pray, therefore, to the God of Peace
that we trample the spirit of evil beneath our feet,
that he may no longer retain human beings captive
and do injury to the House of God.

Offer our prayers to the Most High,
That, without delay, they may draw His mercy down upon us.
Take hold of the dragon, that old serpent,
which is the spirit of evil, bind him,
and cast him into the bottomless pit
so that he should no more seduce the nations.

Amen.

—adapted Catholic prayer, "Prayer to Saint Michael the Archangel"

***

Saint Michael the Archangel,
loyal champion of God and His People,
I turn to you with confidence

and seek your powerful intercession.

For the love of God,
who made you so glorious in grace and power,
and for the love of the Mother of Jesus,
the Queen of the Angels,
be pleased to hear our prayer.

You know the value of our souls in the eyes of God.
May no stain of evil ever disfigure its beauty.
Help us to conquer the evil spirit that tempts us.

We desire to imitate your loyalty to God and the Holy Mother
and your great love for God and people.

And since you are God's messenger for the care of His people,
we entrust to you our most cherished intentions.

Amen.

—traditional Catholic prayer, "Novena to Saint Michael the Archangel"

This Happy Day

Let us all praise Michael,
let none defraud themselves
of today's greatest joy.
This happy day, forever
telling of the holy angels'
solemn victory.

The old dragon is driven off!
His legion, heaven's foe,
is put to flight!
In confusion the confuser
is expelled, the accuser
hurled from heaven's height.

Under Michael's tutelage
there is peace on earth,
peace in heaven—
praise and jubilation.
His courage, full of strength,
defends the communal good,
and triumphs on the battlefield...

—Adam of Saint Victor,
"A Liturgical Poem of Saint Adam the Victor"

Paradise Lost

Goe Michael of Celestial Armies Prince,
And thou in Military prowess next
Gabriel, lead forth to Battel these my Sons
Invincible, lead forth my armed Saints
By Thousands and by Millions rang'd for fight;
Equal in number to that Godless crew
Rebellious, them with Fire and hostile Arms
Fearless assault, and to the brow of Heav'n
Pursuing drive them out from God and bliss,
Into thir place of punishment, the Gulf
Of Tartarus, which ready opens wide
His fiery chaos to receave thir fall.

Michael, this my behest have thou in charge,
Take to thee from among the Cherubim
Thy choice of flaming Warriours, least the Fiend
Or in behalf of Man, or to invade
Vacant possession som new trouble raise:

Hast thee, and from the Paradise of God
Without remorse drive out the sinful Pair,
From hallowd ground th' unholie, and denounce
To them and to thir Progenie from thence
Perpetual banishment.

John Milton

Down from the Stars

Down from the stars come
the bolts of Saint Micha-el,
bringing healing strength
to humankind.

Open your hearts
to receive his power,
helping you do
the very best you can.

In days of old
a dragon was ruling,
forcing all to turn
from the way of light.

> Micha-el gathered
> all his host together,
> threw that dragon
> downright out of sight.

> —traditional Waldorf children's song

***

Saint Michael, heaven's glorious
 commissioner of police,
who once so neatly and successfully
 cleared God's premises
of all its undesirables,
look with kindly and professional eyes
on your earthly force.

Give us cool heads, stout hearts,
an uncanny flair for investigation
and wise judgment.

Make us the terror of burglars,
the friend of children and law-abiding
 citizens,
kind to strangers, polite to bores, strict
 with law-breakers,
and impervious to temptations.

You know, Saint Michael,

from your own experiences with the
 devil,
that the police officer's lot on earth is
 not always a happy one;
but your sense of duty that so pleased
 God,
your hard knocks that so surprised the
 devil,
and your angelic self-control give us
 inspiration.

And when we lay down our nightsticks,
enroll us in your heavenly force,
where we will be as proud to guard the
 throne of God
as we have been to guard the city of
 all the people.

Amen.

—Catholic prayer,
"Police Officer's Prayer to Saint Michael"

***

>Prince of God's host;
>Standard Bearer;
>Mighty Seraph;
>One of the Seven

that stand before the throne;
Dauntless Challenger
whose cry ran through
the vastness of heaven:
"Who is like to God!"

Guardian of God's beloved people;
Glorious Champion of God's House
under the New Law;
Triumphant Defender
of the Woman and her Child;
Vanquisher of the Dragon
and Chainer of his strength;
Leader of souls
into the holy light.

—adapted Catholic prayer,
"Liturgy of the Feast of St. Michael"

The Sacrifice

The Holy One calls you to the mountaintop.

"Bring your only child," he says. "And a sharp knife."

You saddle a donkey for yourself and another for your child. You ride up the steep path at dawn. You stop in a clearing near the summit just as the sun is cresting the slope. You dismount, lift your child into your arms. You give your child dried apples and some hard cheese. You gather downed wood and split it.

"What are you doing?" your child asks.

"The Holy One has told me to offer a sacrifice," you answer.

"But where is the lamb?" the child presses you. "Where is the ram?"

Your eyes fill with tears. "God will provide," you say, but you have a terrible feeling it will not be so simple. That the sacrifice will not be abstract, but inextricably entwined with the blood of your blood. That everything you have ever believed will be shattered by your answer to the divine call.

You take the child by the hand and, eyes half-closed, follow your feet where God guides them. You climb together. There is a subtle drop in temperature and a feeling of spaciousness.

You open your eyes. You have stepped into a clearing. A large slab of stone sits in the center of the leafy chamber.

"Rest here," you say to your child. The child climbs onto the rock and lies down. The eyes of the child grow heavy and soon close.

You clutch your heart, cry out silently.

"What do you want?" you demand of the Holy One.

"All I ask of you is your only child," the voice says.

Your knees buckle and you drop. "Thy will be done," you whisper.

But you do not mean it. You mean, anything but this one, life of my life, cornerstone of my existence. You mean, thy will be done if and only if it conforms with my desires and ideas. You mean, only if it doesn't hurt.

You stumble to your feet. Hoist the bundle of kindling off your back. You lay the firewood all around your sweetly sleeping child. You are blinded by your own tears. You bend to kiss your child, who stirs a little and, without waking, murmurs to you.

You draw your knife and raise it far above your head. You recite every prayer you have ever learned. You call out to God in all his many names. You *are a dancer who has lost her mind and pirouettes to the edge of the cliff, ready to leap into the arms of the void. There is no turning back.*

Just as you are about to plunge the dagger into the heart of your only child, an invisible hand stops your hand. A voice penetrates the terrible silence.

It is the Archangel Michael.

"Lay down your weapon," Michael says. "You have passed the test. Your awe of God exceeds your self-importance."

In that moment, there is a rustling in the bushes surrounding the clearing. An old mountain goat has caught its horns in the thicket. You approach the animal and look into its eyes. The goat nods its gray head. You bow to the creature and slit its throat.

Your child wakes and starts crying at the sight of the blood. The child clamors down from the stone altar and squats beneath a tree on the far end of the clearing, staring at you reproachfully.

You lift the goat in your arms and carry it to the rock. You set its body inside the circle of firewood and ignite it. The pyre bursts into flames, engulfing the sacrificial goat. You stand watch until the body has been consumed and the flames have turned to embers and finally ash.

Your child is asleep again, tears dried in streaks on dirty cheeks. You carry the child back to the place where the donkeys are tethered. When the child wakes, you offer water, figs, and an orange. You tell a story. A singing-story. Your child laughs, snuggles. You are forgiven. You descend the mountain toward home. You will never be the same.

Image 1.1

Chapter Two

The Calling

The Burning Bush

It was the invisible archangel, Michael, who spirited the fugitive Israelite, Moses, away from the angry pharaoh and deep into the desert, where Moses found sanctuary among the tribal people of Midian. There, Moses fell in love with Zipporah, daughter of the sage, Jethro, and settled into the simple life of raising a family and tending his father-in-law's sheep.

One day, overcome by an inexplicable urge to keep moving, Moses guided his flock far into the wilderness. He led them to the summit of the Mountain of God, where they came upon a meadow of tall wild grasses. As Moses stood watching his ecstatic sheep plunge their muzzles into their meal, he thought he heard the crackling of flame.

Alarmed, he scanned for the source of the sound. There, at the edge of the meadow, a high desert plant was on *fire. Moses rushed toward the blaze, prepared to put it out with his cloak, when a voice called to him from within the burning bush. It was the Archangel Michael.*

"Moses," Michael said. And again, "Moses."

"Here I am," said the shepherd.

"Take off your shoes and stay where you are," the angel commanded. "This is holy ground."

The bush continued to burn but remained intact, vibrant, and green beneath the dancing flames. Moses unlaced his sandals and prostrated himself, pressing his forehead against the moist grass. He did not dare to gaze upon an angel of God.

"The Holy One has heard your cries for justice," Michael continued. "He knows how the Children of Israel suffer under the yoke of slavery in Egypt. He has made you his prophet. Go now. Return to the land of the pharaoh, to the city you fled in your youth. Demand that the tyrant let your people go."

"But, who am I? I am no one!" Moses stammered.

"You are no one," Michael agreed. "You are nothing but a hollow reed for God's love."

"But what will I say? I am not a man of words. I have a heavy mouth. My speech drops like stones."

"Who do you think it is that made your mouth, that forms your speech and crafts your vocabulary?" Michael said. "Remember, you are nothing but a conduit for divine love."

Moses rose on his knees. "Please, Michael, send anyone else but me!"

The fire popped softly and the archangel said, "Moses, don't you see? It is precisely because you know that you know nothing that your heart may serve as an empty vessel for the love of the Holy One!"

Moses looked into the face of the fiery angel.

"Stay out of your own way," Michael said. "All will be well. I will be with you."

And the man who knelt down as a shepherd stood up as a prophet and led his people through the narrow straits of bondage to freedom in the Land of Milk and Honey.

***

Bright Cherubim,
you who are allowed a deeper insight
into God's secrets,
dispel the darkness of our souls,
and, by virtue of the Divine Blood,
give that supernatural light to our eyes
that will enable us to understand
the truths of liberation.

—adapted Catholic prayer, "Novena in Honor of St. Michael and All the Holy Angels"

***

Ardent Seraphim,
you who dwell
in the eternal home of love,
unceasingly absorbed in the rays
of the Sun of Justice,
we beg you,
by virtue of the Divine Blood,
to enkindle in our hearts
that holy fire
with which you are consumed.

—adapted Catholic prayer, "Novena in Honor of St. Michael and All the Holy Angels"

***

Heavenly virtues,
who sustain the harmony
of the material creation,
you whose name signifies
"Strength,"
have sympathy for our weakness,
and obtain for us,
by virtue of the Divine Blood,
the grace to bear with patience
the trials of this life.

—adapted Catholic prayer, "Novena in Honor of St. Michael and All the Holy Angels"

***

Mika'il was created by Allah five thousand years after Israfil ["the burning one," angel of the Day of Judgment in Islam].

He has saffron hair from his head to his feet and wings of green topaz.

Each hair has a million faces, and in each face are a million eyes from which fall seventy thousand tears. These become the Kerubim, who lean down over the rain and the flowers and the trees and the fruit.

Mika'il has a million tongues, each speaking a million languages.

Mika'il does not laugh.
—Sophy Burnham

***

The word "angel" denotes a function rather than a nature. Those holy spirits of heaven have indeed always been spirits. They can only be called "angels" when they deliver some message.

Moreover, those who deliver messages of lesser importance are called "angels," and those who proclaim messages of supreme importance are called "archangels."

Whenever some act of wondrous power must be performed, Michael is sent, so that his action and his name may make it clear that no one can do what God does by his superior power.

—Homily by Pope Saint Gregory the Great

***

The first visibility of the invisible God was but an instantaneous flash, and there lay outspread the broad world of angels, throbbing with light, and teeming with innumerous and yet colossal life.

The brightness that silvered them was the reflection of Infinite Beauty. From It and because of It they came. Out of It they drew their marvelous diversity of graces. Their sanctities were but mantles made of Its royal texture. They beautified their natures in Its supernatural streams.

It seemed as if here the procession halted for a moment; or perhaps it was only that the sudden flash of light looked like a momentary halt. The new creatures of God, the first created minds, the final offspring of the Uncreated Mind, were bidden to fall in, and accompany the great Procession. Oh, it was fearful, that first sight outside the immense serenity of God!

Then, truly, too truly, there was a halt, as if homage and obedience were refused. There is a gleam as if of intolerable battle, and a coruscation of archangelic weapons, and Michael's war cry echoing, the first created cry, among the everlasting mountains...
—Frederick William

***

Saint Michael the Archangel, pray for us.
Most glorious attendant of the Triune Divinity,
Standing at the right of the Altar of Incense,
Ambassador of Paradise,
Glorious Prince of the heavenly armies,
Leader of the angelic hosts,
Warrior who thrust the Fallen One into the underworld,
Defender against the wickedness and snares of the spirit of evil,
Standard-bearer of God's host,
Defender of divine glory,
First defender of the dominion of Christ,
Strength of God,
Invincible prince and warrior,

Angel of peace,
Guardian of the Faith,
Guardian of the Legion of Saint Michael,
Champion of God's people,
Champion of the Legion of Saint Michael,
Guardian angel of the Blessed Sacrament,
Defender of God's House,
Defender of the Legion of Saint Michael,
Protector of the Holy Father,
Protector of the Legion of Saint Michael,
Angel of Holy Action,
Powerful intercessor of people of faith,
Bravest defender of those who hope in God,
Guardian of our souls and bodies,
Healer of the sick,
Helper of those in their agony,
Consoler of the souls in limbo,
God's messenger for the souls of the just,
Terror of the evil spirits,
Victorious in battle against evil,
Guardian and Patron of the Universal House of God.

Pray for us, O glorious Saint Michael,

That we may be made worthy of the promises of Christ.

Amen.

> —adapted Catholic prayer

***

Michael!
Exalted, powerful Prince of Heaven,
you bear upward the high golden radiance
of Christ, the King.

Holy is your name,
O Michael
"who is like unto God."

You are Companion of the Thrones;
you are the foundation stone
of the celestial canopy;
you stand in the fortress of the Dominions;
you tower high among the Virtues.
You appear like the radiant light of heaven
among the Powers and Principalities.

You bear the fire of expiation
into the holy choir of the Cherubim,
and, supported by your holy spear,
rule over the Seraphim.

As rightfully befits the eldest,
you lead the army of the heavenly host.
In the fourfold row of the eldest,
you show yourself radiant
in the course of ages.

You are the priest
of the two times two
rulers of the fourth globe.
You stay close to the Creator's throne—
for there is your rightful place.

You are the countenance
of the ninefold hierarchy
of the angelic orders.
And of the noble structure
of the myriad heavenly hosts,
perpetually praising
the thrice Holy Trinity.

You cover the highest Godhead's

face and feet forever,
bowing in exchange
to its three aspects.

Companion of Uriel,
of Gabriel and Raphael,
from the world's beginnings
you have covered the Godhead
with six rushing flames,
brightly blazing.

Truly you will remain, too,
to the end of time
always united to what is necessary.

—Gothic hymn

***

So I remained alone. I saw this great vision. No strength remained in me; my robustness turned to pallor, and I could retain no strength. I hear the sound of his words, and when I heard the sound of his words, I was in a deep sleep upon my face with my face towards the ground.

Behold! a hand touched me and moved me onto my knees and the palms of my hands.

He said to me, "Daniel, greatly beloved man, understand the words that I speak to you, and stand in your place, for I have been sent to you now."

As he spoke these words to me, I stood atremble.

He said to me, "Do not fear, Daniel, for from the first day that you set your heart to understand and to fast before your God, your words have been heard; and I have come because of your words. But the prince of the Persian kingdom stood opposed to me for twenty-one days until Michael, one of the foremost heavenly princes, came to help me, for I had remained there alone beside the kings of Persia ... No one reinforces me against these, except your heavenly prince, Michael..."

—Daniel 10:13-14, 10:21

***

Jacob was left alone and a man wrestled with him until the break of dawn. When he perceived that he could not overcome [Jacob], [the figure] struck the socket of his hip, so that Jacob's hip-socket was dislocated as he wrestled with him.

Then he said, "Let me go, for dawn has broken."

And [Jacob] said, "I will not let you go unless you bless me."

He said to him, "What is your name?"

He replied, "Jacob."

He said, "No longer will it be said that your name is Jacob, but Israel, for you have striven with the Divine and with man and have overcome."

Then Jacob inquired, "Divulge, if you please, your name."

And [the being] said, "Why then do you inquire of my name?" And he blessed him there.

—Genesis 32:25-31

Joshua's Vision of Michael

It happened when Joshua was in Jericho that he raised his eyes and saw, and behold!—a man was standing opposite him with his sword drawn in his hand.

Joshua went toward him and said to him, "Are you with us or with our enemies?"

He said, "No, for I am the commander of Hashem's legion; now I have come."

Joshua fell before him to the ground and prostrated himself, and said to him, "What does my master say to his servant?"

The commander of Hashem's legion said to Joshua, "Remove your shoe from upon your foot, for the place upon which you stand is holy." And Joshua did so.

—Joshua 5:13-15

Joan of Arc: Virgin Warrior

When I was thirteen, I had a voice from God to help me govern myself...

The first time, I was terrified. The voice came to me about noon: It was summer and I was in my father's garden. I had not fasted the day before. I heard the voice on my right and toward the church. There was great light all about. I vowed then to keep my virginity for as long as it should please God.

I saw the light many times before I knew that it was Saint Michael. Afterward, he taught me and showed me such things that I knew it was he.

He was not alone, but duly attended by heavenly angels. I saw them with the eyes of my body as well as I see you. Above all, Saint Michael told me that I must be a good child and that God would help me. He taught me to behave rightly and to go often to Church...

He told me that Saint Catherine and Saint Margaret would come to me, and that I must follow their counsel; that they were appointed to guide and counsel me in what I had to do, and that I must believe what they would tell me, for it was at our Lord's command.

He told me the pitiful state of the Kingdom of France ... Twice and thrice the voice told me that I must depart and go into France. And the voice said that I would raise the siege before

Orleans. And it told me to go to Vaucouleurs, to Robert de Baudricourt, captain of the town, who would give me men to go with me.

And I answered the voice that I was a poor girl who knew nothing of riding and warfare...
—Joan of Arc: A Self-Portrait

***

Whoever is an enemy to Allah and his angels and Messengers, to Gabriel and Michael,—lo! Allah is an enemy to those who reject Faith.
—Qur'an, Surah 2:98

***

There came Our Messengers to Abraham with glad tidings. They said, "Peace!" He answered, "Peace!" and hastened to entertain them with a roasted calf...

And his wife was standing there and she laughed, but [Our Messengers] gave her glad tidings of Isaac, and after him, of Jacob.

She said, "Alas for me! Shall I bear a child, seeing I am an old woman, and my husband here is an old man? That would indeed be a wonderful thing!"

They said, "Do you wonder at Allah's decree? The grace of Allah and His blessings on you, O you people of the house! For He is indeed worthy of all praise, full of all glory!"
—Qur'an, Surah 11:69, 71-73

Abraham and Sarah

All Abraham and Sarah had ever wanted was a child. But, at 100 and 99 years of age, respectively, the couple had long since given up hope of conceiving and had begun to surrender to the process of growing old childless.

Still, from time to time, Sarah became wistful. She would sigh and cup her breasts as if they ached.

Abraham was attuned to his wife's deepest feelings. He sat with her in her quiet grief. Sometimes he stroked her hair.

"What about what the Holy One said to you before he sent us away from

Haran?" Sarah said one evening, as Abraham brought wood for their cook fire and Sarah stacked it outside their tent. The desert night was still and cool.

"Sarah, we've been over this a thousand times."

"But he promised you that your offspring would be as numerous as the stars in the sky. What became of these invisible progeny?"

"The will of the Holy One is inscrutable," Abraham reminded her. But, to Sarah, this piece of religious philosophy had begun to ring hollow. The next day, Abraham was resting from the noontime heat under a tree outside his tent. He noticed three shimmering figures crest the horizon and begin their slow approach toward Sarah and Abraham's compound. They appeared to glitter like daytime stars, and the effusion surrounding them looked almost like wings.

Abraham's heart surged with joy. Life was lonely in the desert and visitors were always a blessing.

"Welcome, my brothers!" Abraham leapt to his feet and called out to them *as soon as they drew near enough to hear him.*

The travelers all raised a hand in the universal gesture of peace. Each man seemed to have grown from a different branch of the human family. One had an olive complexion and tight brown curls. Another had straight black hair and upward-slanting eyes. The third had rippling gold hair and bronzed skin.

"Come, take shelter with us," said the old man. "You must be tired. Here, a little water to wash your feet." He held out a dipper.

The men nodded gratefully and sat cross-legged beneath the tree. Abraham noticed that none of them carried a burden, and he wondered how they survived the desert empty-handed.

"Where is Sarah?" the man with the golden hair asked.

"Sarah, my love, we have company!" Abraham did not seem to notice that the stranger knew his wife's name. "Come! Bring tea and honey cakes."

Sarah pushed aside the flap of the tent and stared at the strangers until her eyes adjusted to the daylight. Then she gasped and stepped back.

"What?" Abraham was mortified. "Sarah, where are your manners?"

"These are not men, Abraham. They are angels. They have been sent by God."

Abraham prostrated himself and then rose only to his knees.

"That one is Gabriel," Sarah said. "He is charged with destroying Sodom and Gomorrah."

"Sodom?" Abraham said. "Gomorrah? What about the innocent people who live there?"

"I will spare the righteous," Gabriel said.

"And that one is Raphael," Sarah continued. "He disguised himself as the man who healed you last year."

Abraham pressed his hands together in gratitude. Raphael smiled and nodded.

"And this one," Sarah spoke as she held the third man's gaze, "is Michael."

As his true identity was revealed, the Archangel Michael rose to his feet. He spoke to Abraham, but he continued to look at Sarah. "Your wife shall have a son."

A burst of laughter bubbled from Sarah's belly. She tried to cover her mouth. That's ridiculous, she thought to herself. I am far too old, and my husband is even older!

"Why are you laughing?" Michael asked. "I am an angel of the Holy One. Is there anything the Holy One cannot do?"

"I didn't laugh!" Sarah said, embarrassed.

"You did," Michael insisted. "But it does not matter. At this time next year, I will visit you again and you will be suckling a son. And you shall call him Isaac, in remembrance of your laughter."

Sarah shook her head in wonderment and went inside to prepare tea.

After they had refreshed themselves, the angels rose and thanked the couple for their hospitality. Abraham walked with them a little way into the desert, then leaned on his staff and watched them dip back over the horizon. He thought he saw a flash of wings as they disappeared.

Image 2.1

Chapter Three

Guardian of Souls

Balance

Michael, when it is my time to leave this world, please collect my soul and deliver me straight into the arms of my Beloved. Do not let me attempt that journey alone.

What do I know about navigating the landscape of the dead? What if the fearsome demons of my unfinished business petrify me, turn me to ice and shatter me? What if the promise of sensual gratification lures me back into another incarnation?

Michael, all I have ever wanted is to merge with my Beloved, lover transfigured in Beloved, so that nothing remains but love.

I may lose my way without you, Michael. I cannot risk losing my way.

They say you will come again, Michael, when the cosmos runs its course and readies itself for collapse. That you will gather the souls of the righteous and the wicked, place us on your great scales and weigh our deeds. That if we have been loving and kind, you will take the key from around your neck and open the gates of Paradise, inviting us to live there forever.

And that if we have been selfish and cruel, it is you who will banish us.

I have been greedy and covetous, Michael. I have criticized children, taken naps when bills were due, exaggerated my credentials. I have gossiped and cursed. I have turned away from the suffering of others.

But I have also suffered.

I have yielded to The Way Things Are. Opened my broken heart to love again when everything and everyone I love was taken from me. Determined to love even more.

May I sit lightly in your measuring cup, my angel.

***

> In a dream I marked him there,
> With his fire-gold flickering hair,
> In his blinding armor stand,
> And the scales were in his hand;
> Mighty were they, and full well

They could poise both heaven and hell...
In one scale I saw him place
All the glories of our race,
Cups that lit Belshazzar's feast,
Gems the wonder of the East,
Kublai's scepter, Caesar's sword,
Many a poet's golden word,
Many a skill of science vain
To make men as gods again.

In the other scale he threw
Things regardless, outcast, few,
Martyr-ash, arena-sand,
Of Saint Francis' cord a strand,
Disillusions and despairs
Of young saints with grief-grayed hairs,
Broken hearts that break for man.
Marvel through my pulses ran
Seeing then the beam divine
Swiftly on this hand decline.
While earth's splendor and renown
Mounted light as thistle down...

—James Russell Lowell, "St. Michael the Weigher"

***

You, O Michael,
are the protector of our souls
in their passage from time to
eternity.
During this present life,
you keep your eye on our needs
and your ear open to our prayers.
Though awed by the brightness of
your glory,
we love you, dear prince of
heaven,
and we live happily and contented
beneath the shadow of your wings.
In a few years, perhaps,
our community will be uttering
their prayers
over our lifeless remains.
They will ask God to deliver us
from the lion's mouth
and request that the one who
carries the banner of truth,
Saint Michael,
bring us into the holy light.
Watch over us now,
O holy archangel.
Help us to earn your protection.

—adapted Catholic prayer, "The Liturgical Year"

***

Glorious Saint Michael,
guardian and defender of Christ's House,
come to the assistance of His followers,
against whom the powers of hell are unchained.
Guard with special care our Holy Father
and our spiritual guides,
all our monastics and householders,
and especially the children.

Saint Michael, watch over us during life,
defend us against the assaults of the demon,
and assist us especially at the hour of death.
Help us achieve the happiness
of beholding God face-to-face for all eternity.
Amen.

Saint Michael, intercede for me with God
in all my necessities,

Obtain for me a favorable outcome in the matter I confide in you.
Mighty prince of the heavenly host, and victor over rebellious spirits, remember me for I am weak
and likely to miss the mark,
and so prone to pride and ambition.

Be for me, I pray,
my powerful aid in temptation and difficulty,
and above all, do not forsake me in my last struggle with the powers of evil.
Amen.

—adapted Catholic prayer, "Novena Prayer to St. Michael the Archangel"

***

St. Michael, the Archangel!
Glorious Prince;
Leader and Champion
of the heavenly hosts;
Guardian of the souls of humanity;
Vanquisher of the rebel angels!

How beautiful you are
in your celestial armor.
We love you,
sweet Prince of Heaven!

We, your lucky followers,
yearn to earn your special
protection.
Please, ask God to grant us a
share
of your hearty courage.
Pray that we may
cultivate a strong and tender love
for our Emancipator;
And, in every danger or
temptation,
be invincible
against the enemy of our souls.

O paragon of our liberation!
Be with us in our last moments,
And, when our souls escape
this earthly exile,
carry them safely
to the seat of the Ultimate Justice,
where our Lord and Master
might commission you
to swiftly bear us
to the realm of eternal bliss.

Teach us to continuously repeat
your sublime cry:
"Who is like God?"

Amen

—adapted Catholic prayer, "Prayer to
St. Michael Archangel"

**

And after that it came to pass
that my spirit was translated
and it ascended into the heavens
and I saw the Holy Sons of God.

They were stepping on flames of
fire:
their garments were white,
and their faces shone like snow.

And I saw two streams of fire,
and the light of that fire
shone like a hyacinth,
and I fell on my face
before the Lord of Spirits.

And the Archangel Michael
seized me by my right hand,

and lifted me up
and showed me
all the secrets of righteousness.

And he showed me all the secrets
of the ends of the heaven,
and all the chambers of all the stars,
and all the luminaries,
whence they proceed
before the face
of the Holy One.

And he translated my spirit
into the heaven of the heavens,
And I saw there as it were
a structure built of crystals,
and between these crystals
tongues of living fire...

—Book of Enoch, 15

Colors of the Earth

"Michael, I send you now to the four corners of the earth to collect four colors of clay. From this rainbow of materials, I will create humanity in all its diversity."

"They will be beautiful, God."

"They will be glorious!"

***

"They will not be like you and the other angels, Michael. The angels have no choice but to worship me. Human beings will have free will. They can take me or leave me."

"Why would you make creatures who could choose to leave you, God?"

"Curiosity, Michael. I'm eager to see what they do with the gift of freedom. Aren't you?"

***

"Michael, you are troubled. Tell me about it."

"I can't bear the thought of anyone rejecting you, God."

"Then help guide the souls of these new ones onto the path of loving me."

***

"You understand, Michael, that this mission will close the distance between *you and humanity. They will have special access to you."*

"I accept the intimacy, God."

"But they will deeply honor you, Michael, and honoring you, they will honor me. They will consider you a saint, as if you were merely a holier version of them."

"One of them, God?"

"Yes, that's how close they will feel to you. They will call you Saint Michael, and you will continuously reveal yourself to them, the reflection of the divine mystery unfolding forever in their midst."

Image 3.1

Chapter Four

Compassion

Adam and Eve

"I don't think they meant any harm, God." "But, Michael, I specifically told them not to pick that fruit. I had a plan for that fruit."

"You also told me that you created them with free will, God, and that you were curious about what they would do with it."

"Yes."

"Are they still banished, then? Would you consider letting them back into Eden?"

God smiled. "Now I'm curious what they'll do on earth. Aren't you?"

"Yes, God." Michael sighed.

***

"You seem troubled, Michael. Tell me about it."

"I'm afraid they'll perish there, God. They don't know anything about survival. In Eden, everything they needed was within their easy grasp."

"Including the knowledge of good and evil," God pointed out ruefully.

***

"God?"
"Yes, Michael?"
"Can't I help them out a bit? Just give them a little push to get started?"
"Oh, Michael, your heart is vast!"
"And who made me this way?"

***

"Alright, Michael. Go to them."

***

The archangel descended to earth and found the man and woman shivering beneath a fig tree, clinging to one another. They were famished.

Michael picked some of the broad leaves of the tree, demonstrated how to stitch them together, and draped them as garments over the naked bodies of the humans. They stopped shivering.

He plucked the ripe black fruit of the tree and offered it to them.

Gratefully, they ate and were strengthened.

Then Michael taught them how to erect a shelter to keep out the wind and let in the light. He instructed them in cultivating the land and harvesting crops. He showed them how to dig roots from the forest and draw water from the springs hidden in the rocks. He reminded them to offer their prayers of gratitude to every creature whose life they take to sustain their own lives.

***

One night, Michael took Adam on a tour of heaven in his fiery chariot.

Adam was dazzled. "When can we come and live here, Michael?" he asked.

"When your time on earth is finished, Adam."

"When will that be?"

"That's up to God."

"Do you think he'll take us back, Michael? I mean, after what we did in our rebellious youth?"

"Of course, he will, Adam. It's the job of the young to rebel. Don't you think God understands that? Who do you think designed them that way?" The

archangel smiled reassuringly at the man. But his heart was uneasy.

***

Adam and Eve lived simply and sustainably on the earth. They raised children and grew old, contented with life's every day blessings.

When it came time for Adam's death, Michael approached God. "I'm going to get Adam," he said.

"Wait," said God.

Michael paused.

"Adam defied me."

"But it was a learning experience, God. He learned. They both did. And they've used their lessons to live righteously ever since."

"I'm supposed to ignore the fact that they plucked the fruit of knowledge of good and evil? I'm supposed to excuse their supreme arrogance in presuming to see as God sees?"

"It wasn't all their fault, God. It was that damned serpent!"

"They allowed themselves to become defiled."

"I will cleanse them, God! I will dip Adam's soul in the fourth celestial lake

and make him worthy to behold your face. He will be beautiful, God, as you made him."

God's eyes filled with tears.

"He misses you, God," Michael whispered.

"I miss him, too. Go, Michael. Bring the man home."

***

Thee, Michael, thee,
When sight and breathing fail,
The disembodied soul shall see.

The pardoned soul
With solemn joy shall hail,
When holiest rites are spent,
And tears no more avail.

—John Henry

***

O Michael fierce,
Thou king of the angels,
Shield thy people
With the power of thy sword,
Shield thy people
With the power of thy sword.

Spread thy wing
Over sea and land,
East and west,
And shield us from the foe,
East and west,
And shield us from the foe.

Brighten thy feast
From heaven above;
Be with us in the pilgrimage
And in the twistings of the fight;
Be with us in the pilgrimage
And in the twistings of the fight.

Thou chief of chiefs,
Thou chief of the needy,
Be with us in the journey
And in the gleam of the river;
Be with us in the journey
And in the gleam of the river.

Thou chief of chiefs,
Thou chief of angels,
Spread thy wings
Over sea and land,
For thine is their fullness,
Thine is their fullness,
Thine own is their fullness,
Thine own is their fullness.

—oral Celtic prayer

***

Oh, Beloved, the glory of the angel choirs!
Blessed maker and redeemer of humanity!
Help us to one day reach
those bright abodes
and rest in your infinite mercy.

Angel of Peace! O Michael!
Come down from above
and dwell with us in our homes.
Banish wars with all their tears and blood.
Send them back to their native hell.

Angel of Strength! O Gabriel!
Cast out your ancient adversaries,
usurpers of your authority.
Revisit the temples of your triumph
all over the world.

And Raphael, healer of the soul!
Descend from your pure chambers of light.

Cure our diseases.
Correct our dubious course
and guide us back onto the right path.

You, too, beautiful Virgin,
Daughter of the skies!
Mother of light,
Queen of Peace! Come;
Bring the radiant throng of heaven with you
to support us and defend us.

Blessed Creator;
And you, O Word of God,
O Eternal Child, eternally born into this world;
And you, O Holy Spirit,
emanating from both, whose glory fills the earth:
Shower your grace upon us all!

Amen.

—adapted Catholic prayer, the Office of St. Michael

***

Glorious Prince of the heavenly hosts
and subduer of evil spirits,
be mindful of me
who am so fragile and forgetful
and yet so easily swayed
by pride and ambition.

I implore you to dispense
your potent remedy
to innoculate me against
every temptation and difficulty.

Above all,
please do not forsake me
in my final struggle
with the powers of evil.

Amen.

—traditional Catholic prayer, "A Prayer to St. Michael"

***

Yet the Archangel Michael, when he argued with the devil in a dispute over the body of Moses, did not venture to

pronounce a reviling judgment upon him but said, "May the Lord rebuke you!"
—Jude 1:9

***

"...I have come to make you understand what will befall your people in the End of Days, for there is yet a vision for those days...

"...At that time Michael will stand, the great heavenly prince who stands in support of the members of your people, and there will be a time of trouble such as there had never been since there was a nation until that time. But at that time your people will escape; everything that is found written in this book will occur."
—Daniel 12:1

Saint Michael

> If it had not been
> for the child in me
> I would never have
> fallen asleep with
> Saint Michael in the room.

I dreamt of lies
and revelation beasts
eating me alive.
I dreamt of Antichrist
who keeps me locked in towers
all regulation and stiff law.

I woke to find one arm
raised high above my head
holding what,
I didn't know...
Michael had put his sword into
my hand and gently said:
"This is Truth to cut through
these lies, and the Blood
of the Lamb is the only armor
given to children of the Kingdom."

If it had not been
for the child in me
I would have seen that
blazing autumn tree only
as nature's last fire;
I could have missed
his wings tipped around
the edges burning vermillion.

—Father William Hart McNichols

Saint Michael Takes His Time

Michael: Who Is Like God?
At that time there shall arise Michael, the great prince, guardian of your people;
It shall be a time unsurpassed in distress since nations began until that time.
—Daniel 12:1a

Is it time? The little hand trembles
While the big hand wipes away tears.
Is this enough distress?
I am not yet old and I have witnessed
Cold war, hot war, terror and anti-terror terror.
Is it time?
Clock strikes.
Air strikes.
When will Michael strike?
And whose side are you on?
Will you wield the scalpel
Or the sword?

Do angels run late?
Or do they, like their Master, run humble?
Have you emptied yourself into our maimed hands,
Waiting for the moment
When the small hand steadies,
The big hand lands on Now,
And our stricken hearts strike the hour
Of dragonfall, swordmelt,
And the rejoicing cry:
Who is like to You O God?

—Father David M. Denny

***

From the sun which lives afar
To the light within our hearts
Peace does dwell
All is well
Be with us Saint Micha-el.

—A Waldorf children's song

The Abode of Michael

Michael carried his bowl across the great plain of the fourth heaven. A vast white lake glimmered in the near distance. This was the pool in which the archangel dipped the souls of those who had missed the mark during their life on earth. The celestial waters washed them clean.

The meadow was covered with flowers. As he walked, Michael picked the blossoms and dropped them into his bowl. Every flower was a prayer from an angel, which Michael would deliver to God. After his visit with the Holy One, Michael would return with a quantity of oil for each angel, in proportion to the depth and breadth of the angel's devotion.

Overhead, a thousand species of birds sang a thousand love songs. These birds were not actually birds; they were souls created to perpetually sing the praises of the Creator.

As Michael gazed upward at these magnificent beings, he noticed a man standing outside the gates of the fifth heaven. It was the prophet Baruch. He *was waiting to pass from the fourth into the fifth realm of paradise. Baruch sat very still, lost in silent prayer.*

"I'll be right there!" *the archangel called, moved by the prophet's patience and serenity. He unfolded his great angel wings and lifted himself into the sky.*

"Michael, you've come!" *Baruch rose to his feet and embraced the archangel in gratitude.*

"Of course. Why didn't you just call me?"

"I didn't feel worthy of bothering you, Michael."

"Which is exactly what makes you so worthy," *Michael said, kissing the prophet's cheek.*

He unclasped his key from his belt, inserted it into the heavenly gate, and flung it wide.

"Welcome home, my friend!"

Pure white light unfurled across the threshold like a bank of summer mist pouring into a cove. Baruch stepped into the divine radiance and became one with it.

Image 4.1

Closing Prayer

O holy Archangel Michael,
be with me.
Protect me from my own false self,
which tempts me with comfortable ignorance
and threatens to lull me to sleep.
Call me to my God-self,
radiant and wise.
Call and call again.

Defend me, too, against
the forces of darkness in the world around me.
Help me to discern that which is truly negative
from that which merely threatens my complacency.
Shield me in the shadow of your vast wings,
so that I may take refuge and grow strong.
Then, let me be a beacon of light and justice
to a world struggling for true righteousness.

O chief of the tribe of angels,
place your sword of unconditional love
in my hand.
Give me the courage
to cut through illusion
and set the truth free.
Let me wield this divine weapon
with clarity and compassion.
Let me be fierce and humble.
Let me place the greatest good
of all who suffer
above my own comfort.

O Prince of Light,
when my time comes
to leave this world of form
and return to my divine source,
carry me
as you have carried my ancestors
since the creation of humankind
home to the Supreme Light
that gives birth to us all
and lovingly receives our souls
when our work is finished.

Amen.

—Mirabai Starr

Sources

"St Michael, the archangel of God..." by Father Emmanuel Kaniamparampil

"O glorious archangel..." adapted prayer by Mirabai Starr

"Glorious St. Michael..." in "Prayer for Help Against Spiritual Enemies" from www.marysremnant.org

"O Word of God!..." from www.catholic-forum.com

Revelation 12:7-8 from *The New American Bible*

"Most glorious Prince..." in "Prayer to Saint Michael the Archangel" from www.catholic-forum.com

"Saint Michael the Archangel..." in "Novena to Saint Michael the Archangel" from www.catholic-forum.com

"This Happy Day" from *The Archangel Michael*

From John Milton's *Paradise Lost*

"Down from the Stars" from Waldorf School curriculum

"Police Officer's Prayer to Saint Michael" from www.marysremnant.org

"Prince of God's host..." from *St. Michael and the Angels*

(top) "Bright Cherubim..." in "Novena in Honor of St. Michael and All the Holy Angels" from *St. Michael and the Angels*

(bottom) "Ardent Seraphim..." in "Novena in Honor of St. Michael and All the Holy Angels" from *St. Michael and the Angels*

"Heavenly virtues..." in "Novena in Honor of St. Michael and All the Holy Angels" from *St. Michael and the Angels*

"Mike'il was created..." from *A Book of Angels*

Homily by Pope Saint Gregory the Great from www.catholic-forum.com

"The first visibility..." from *St. Michael and the Angels*

"St. Michael the Archangel, pray for us..." from www.2heartsnetwork.com

"Michael! Exalted,..." Gothic hymn from *The Archangel Michael*

"So I remained alone..." from *The Torah*

"Jacob was left alone..." from *The Torah*

"Joshua's Vision of Michael" from *The Torah*

"Joan of Arc: Virgin Warrior" from *The Archangel Michael*

"Whoever is an enemy..." from *The Qur'an*

Page 70:"There came Our Messengers..." from *The Qur'an*

"St. Michael the Weigher" from *The Complete Poetical Works of James Russell Lowell*

"You, O Michael..." in "The Liturgical Year" adapted by Mirabai Starr

"Glorious St. Michael..." in "Novena in Honor of St. Michael and All the Holy Angels" from www.marysremnant.org

"St. Michael, the Archangel!..." in "Prayer to St. Michael Archangel" from www.marysremnant.org

Book of Enoch, 15 from *The Archangel Michael*

"Thee, Michael, thee..." from *St. Michael and the Angels*

Celtic prayer from *Carmina Gadelica*

"O, Beloved, the glory..." adapted by Mirabai Starr

"Glorious Prince..." in "A Prayer to St. Michael" from www.marysremnant.org

(top) Jude 1:9 from *The New American Bible*

(bottom) Daniel 12:1 from *The Torah*

"Saint Michael" from *Fire Above, Water Below*

"Saint Michael Takes His Time" by Father David M. Denny

Children's Waldorf song by Jenna Paulden

Bibliography

Books

Bamford, Christopher and Rudolf Steiner. *The Archangel Michael.* Great Barrington, MA: SteinerBooks, 1996.

Burnham, Sophy. *A Book of Angels.* New York: Ballantine Books, 2004.

Carmichael, Alexander, ed. *Carmina Gadelica.* Edinburgh, Scotland: Floris Books, 2004.

Lowell, James Russell. *The Complete Poetical Works of James Russell Lowell.* Whitefish, Montana: Kessinger Publishing, 2005.

McNichols, William Hart. *Fire Above, Water Below.* Unpublished.

Milton, John. *Paradise Lost.* New York: Penguin Classics, 2003.

The New American Bible. Iowa Falls, Iowa: World Bible Publishers, 1987.

The Qur'an. New York: Tahrike Tarsile Qur'an, Inc., 2003.

Steiner, Rudolf. *Michaelmas and the Soul Forces of Man.* Spring Valley, New York: Anthroposophic Press, 1946.

St. Michael and the Angels. Rockford, Illinois: Tan Books and Publishers, 1986.

The Tanach (Torah): The Artscroll Series. New York: Mesorah Publications, 1996.

Websites

www.marysremnant.org

www.catholic-forum.com

www.catholic.org

www.2heartsnetwork.com

Credits

Text Credits

Traditional Catholic prayer on page 29 reprinted by permission of its author, Father Emmanuel Kaniamparampil.

Excerpts as submitted from *Enduring Grace: Living Portraits of Seven Women Mystics* by Carol Lee Flinders © 1993 by Carol Lee Flinders. Reprinted by permission of HarperCollins Publishers.

Excerpt from *A Book of Angels* by Sophy Burnham © 2004 by Sophy Burnham reprinted by permission of Sophy Burnham.

"Saint Michael" page 102-103 reprinted by permission of Father William Hart McNichols.

"Saint Michael Takes His Time" page 104-105 reprinted by permission of Father David M. Denny.

Excerpts from *The Archangel Michael* by Rudolf Steiner and Christopher Bamford © 2005 reprinted by permission of Steiner Books.

Excerpts from *St. Michael and the Angels* © 2005 reprinted by permission of Tan Books, Rockford, Illinois.

Art Credits

14th century icon of Archangel Michael in the Byzantine Museum in Athens, Greece. © Robert Harding Picture Library Ltd/Alamy

19th century color woodcut private collection. © INTERFOTO Pressebildagentur/Alamy

Statue of St. Michael on the top of Castel Sant' Angelo in Rome, Italy. © Ronald Sumners/Shutterstock

Moses and the burning bush. © Lebrecht Music and Arts Photo Library/Alamy

St. Michael the Archangel fighting a dragon with a sword c1484-1526. © The Print Collector/Alamy

The statue of Archangel Michael in Rome, Italy. © Ronald Sumners/Shutterstock

Archangel Michael Fresco from Rila Monastery, Bulgaria. © Ivo Vitanov Velinov/Shutterstock

About Sounds True

Sounds True was founded in 1985 with a clear vision: to disseminate spiritual wisdom. Located in Boulder, Colorado, Sounds True publishes teaching programs that are designed to educate, uplift, and inspire. We work with many of the leading spiritual teachers, thinkers, healers, and visionary artists of our time.

To receive a free catalog of tools and teachings for personal and spiritual transformation, please visit www.soundstrue.com, call toll-free 800-333-9185, or write to us at the address below.

SOUNDS TRUE
PO BOX 8010 / BOULDER, CO 80306

Front Cover Flap

Who is the Archangel Michael? Never unkind, but not always gentle, he embodies the essence of the "spiritual warrior"—courageous and strong in the face of injustice or illusion, a ceaseless devotee of truth. *Saint Michael* offers you the hand of this protective force through a collection of prayers, scripture, contemplations, and stories that span the ages and traditions in which this legendary figure has appeared.

The name Michael means "who is like God." By invoking Michael's power, we invite into our own lives the divine energy to lift us past obstacles. *Saint Michael* gives you a devotional treasure for calling on this archangel for protection in times of danger, for strength in taking action for the greater good, for compassion in defense of the innocent, and for grace as we embark on the journey that awaits at the end of our lives.

Back Cover Flap

Saint Michael
THE ARCHANGEL

...appears in spiritual traditions across the globe, from Judaism to Christianity to Islam. His roles include the guardian angel of the children of Israel, the patron saint of warriors, and the transporter of souls.

***

MIRABAI STARR teaches philosophy and world religions at the University of New Mexico, and is the author of new translations of *Dark Night of the Soul* by John of the Cross and The Interior Castle and *The Book of My Life* by Teresa of Avila. She lives in Taos.

Back Cover Material

Saint Maichael THE ARCHANGEL

***

Under Michael's tutelage there is peace on earth, peace in heaven—praise and jubilation. His courage, full of strength, defends the communal good..."
Rudolf Steiner

www.ingramcontent.com/pod-product-compliance
Lightning Source LLC
Chambersburg PA
CBHW061958220426
43662CB00011B/1737